I Still Pretend You're Here

*To Jonathan
Thank you my
Friend
Peter Velatti*

I Still Pretend You're Here

Grieving and Healing Through Poetry

A Father surviving the Loss of His Son at a Young Age, the love of his life and her son, through poetry.

Peter Velotti

Amazon Books

NEW YORK

IN MEMORY OF AND DEDICATED TO

Peter Louis Velotti, my son, Mary Alice Miller, my fiancé, Jermaine Miller, my stepson, Doris Bursee, my mother-in-law., Charlie Giardino, my childhood friend.

RICHARD RANSONE III   MIKE LAVAIA

Table of Contents

Forward vii
Acknowledgments & Special Thanks viii
Introduction 10
That Glorious Voice 11
Pity The Children 13
You Put A Smile On Gods Face 15
Farewell To The Captain 17
Trayvon Goes Out For A Walk 19
Acrostic Poetry 21
Alone And Out Of Sight 23
From Her Eyes To Mine 25
Honor Our Memorial Day 27
I Feel Your Love Wherever I Go 29
Sitting In A Lonely Room 30
Its Time To Say Goodbye 32
To Distinguish The Four Seasons 34
Why Is Everybody Always Picking On Me 36
Old Photos And Other Things 37
Still Looking Gorgeous To Me 39
Stand Up To What'S Right 41
Close Friends Are Family To Me 43
The Loudest Noise Is Silence 45

Oh Lord Can'T I Ever Go Home 47
Oh Lord Can'T I Ever Go Home (Continued).. 49
Dedicated To My Niece Anna Liga 50
Dedicated To My Second Wife Sonia Alva Velotti 51
Is It Really Over? 53
Is It Just Coincidental? 55
Is It Just Coincidental? (Continued) 57
Now Stop The Madness 59
I Love You Dad 63
Respected And Appreciated 64
Respected And Appreciated (Continued) 66
Mysterious 68
Where Are The So Called Fathers 70
My Grandchildren 72
We All Must Unite 74
Found Together 76
I Pretend You'Re Still Here 77
I Still Pretend You'Re Here (Continued) 79
Us Three Were Pure Gold 80
My Stepsons By My Side 82
My Stepsons By My Side (Continued) 84
My Two Hero'S 86
My Two Hero'S (Continued) 88
My Two Hero'S (Continued) 91

Pride	93
Pride (Continued)	95
About The Author	97

FORWARD

This Book is for any parents that has lost a child to cancer early, to any spouse or lover, that has lost a love suddenly.

Losing a partner can be devastating and can keep us stuck in a cycle of depression and loneliness. Losing a child early, for any reason, can seem unbearable. Your children are your greatest legacy.

How do we move forward after so much pain? In our service to others and sharing our pain through our gifts, we often find our healing and strength.

When my friend Peter shared his pain from so much lost, I advised him, using my counseling skills, to work it out through writing.

I Knew he had a gift of words and that if he could just put it all on paper, they would still be gone, but through service of helping others in his writing, his pain would become bearable and in that, he would help others who have lost their children, spouses and family.

Peter has one goal, to help others work through their pain by sharing their gifts.

If you lost a major love in your life, a child or anyone dear, find your gift, use it to help others going through the same thing, and in that, you will find healing and keep their memory alive forever.

Thank you my friend, for trusting me with your pain and your gift.

Tanya Rochester Cooper

ACKNOWLEDGMENTS & SPECIAL THANKS

Special thanks to my lady Mary Alice Williams Miller

R.I.P to my dear friends: Charlie Giardino, Mary A. Miller, Nick Giardino, Jermaine Miller, Alvin, (Monty), Montero, Doris Burcee.

Thank you to all who helped me during my losses, I could not have got through without your love, understanding, kindness and support.

A special thanks to:

Rubin Casado, George Czerniewski, Jason Medina, John Cuva, Anna Liga, Natasha Agard, Jalin Miller, Sonia Alva Velotti, Frank & Maryann Prudenti, Bob & Lucille Cosenza, Martinez Sisters, Randy Perillo, Jennifer Velotti, My Pelham Bay LL Player On those Field Of Dreams,

O.L.A Class Of 1986.

Garito Manor Staff, for keeping us all safe. My Post Office Family - R. Rivera, T. Mims & Godson, Carmelo M. Aponte, Dennis Drijon, Frank Springman, Haydee Brugas, (For being there when it counted), Charlie Cristiano - Best gift ever, of my lady. Louie Ferrina - Donation in honor of my son, John Figaro - All our gigs together & the big hit.

My Poetry & Acting teacher, Carol Hebold, Writer Actor Chris Raffaele & Tim Cinnante, Brendan Evers - Greatest compliment, (your son was the most genuine person I ever knew).

Families - Velotti - Liga - Russo - Perillo - Bursee - Graney - Distefano - Miller - Williams - Agard

- Love you all!

VERY SPECIAL THANKS - TANYA ROCHESTER COOPER

A dear close friend & sweet lady whose patience, time and effort & kick ass attitude helped so very much with typing and listening. Her work, (Put A Smile On God's Face).

She is Director at FosterKidsUnite, Inc, Producer, Talk Show Host, "On The Town". You hold a dear place in my heart, God bless

Introduction

I met Peter through a fellow comedian. He delivered the most memorable poem to our foster youth and myself at one of FosterKidsUnite, Inc fundraisers.

The words that rang out on that page touched everyones heart. Peter has a gift with words, words can heal.

This book of poetry will remind us all how vulnerable we all are to losing loved ones.

In the end, it is the legacy we leave, the words that are written onto pages, formed into a book, that will keep the memory alive of those we loved and lost.

That Glorious Voice

Whitney, you became the number one pop singer hit after hit, everything seemed to fit.

At the Super Bowl you sang the National Anthem crowd went wild, America felt so very proud.

For you acting wasn't hard, you were splendid in the Bodyguard. You with your sweet charms, Kevin Costner held you in his arms. Love was evident for you two, when you sang "I Always Love You".

That angelic voice and beautiful face slowly changed Diane Sawyer asked something's wrong, You said don't worry Jesus loves me I'm very strong, oh Whitney you were so so wrong.

TV and Magazines were putting you down, don't these critics notice theirs also tears in the eyes of a clown.

I am ok don't worry about me, foolishly too blind to see.

Your voice got worse you looked so thin, what a shame what a sin. Mom pleased on the phone, we love you please come home.

News flash the world was told, Whitney is dead at 45 years old.

In church a moving speech by Tyler Perry, the bible tells us Whitney's gone home be merry. Kevin Costner mentions Whitney's fear, while his eyes tear.

Stevie Sang "*Ribbon In The Sky*", while her mom cried, "oh lord why"? You said you were tuff, shame is you did not love yourself enough.

Oh God we had no choice, we will always love that glorious voice.

Pity The Children

In memory of the Sandy Hook children

See you later love you and then you kiss your child on the cheek, typical school day each and Every week.

A little later on someone shouts "a maniac at our school has gone wild", you freeze and wonder oh God not my child.

No this can't be, oh Lord please please hear my plea.

When I get there and see friends waiting for their daughters and sons, we later learn 26 are Killed by his guns.

Now the awful wait while the police go over clues, and when parents get the awful news. Now on TV we hear how the principle was so brave and lost her life for the children she tried to save.

We are told evil came today at our beautiful place, let's ask ourselves is anywhere truly safe? Unlike us today's kids listen to the so-called music that preaches the degradation of woman And to a kill cop, when will this stupidity stop.

How movies and video games gets blown up and praises evil and guns, it's the brainwashing for some of our daughters and sons.

At the crime scene the news is read, twenty-six little angels are dead. Oh God the horror of it all, while the tears fall.

When you lose a child that pain never goes away, and the nightmares continue to stay. This is why we need strength and have faith, while the Lord greets each child at heaven's gate

You Put A Smile On Gods Face

Dedicated to Tanya Rochester Cooper and FosterKidsUnite, Inc.

She was abused by two foster brothers who were evil, her life was truly unbelievable Tanya truly knows the ups and downs of life, being a foster child you face so much strife. She's been fortunate to have foster parents and nuns who care, also others who brought so much hopelessness and despair.

As a young girl.

She faced hunger and was penniless, which brought her to homelessness.

Tanya prayed for her brother Coop the closet person in her life would never be apart, sadly many years later he passed spiritually Coop will always live in her heart.

This lady is a fighter, her life became much brighter. She became a fashion model, working in Italy and France, now overjoyed in a tranquil trance.

Later became a mother of two girls whom she brags about, her love for them has no doubt. Today she's a Director of foster kids always on the go, even has her own podcast and Youtube show.

Tanya also wrote a book on foster care, it's informative teaching about life and who to fear. When it comes to loving her foster children she has events as a host, my dear friend is always their when it counts most.

This lady of class and grace, puts a smile on God's face.

Farewell To The Captain

New York Yankees gave you a start Derek you gave the fans your heart.

You lived your dream, always gave the right answers its not about me only the team. Never cheated the game and played hard, unlike the steroid phony A-rod.

Rizzuto praised your talent with lots of wows, and clutch hitting with holy cows. True Yankee fans always rooted for you, even in a slump they would never boo. Young ladies never wanted you to wed, fame never went to your head.

Every at bat the fans would shout, winning is what you were all about. Our city treated you like a King, knowing you gave your all for the ring.

All-Star year after year, gutsy diving catch into the stands showing no fear. Out of position you roamed, tossing runner out at home.

Always hustle never lag, winning New York another flag.

Joe Torre loved you like a son, cried on your 3,000 hit a home run.

Announce your retirement, surprisingly Red Sox fans show respect not resentment. Yogi states "Derek makes us proud" another Yankee name, in the Hall of Fame.

Derek Jeter's last game some fans say a prayer showing their faith, Bernie-Tino-Jorya-Andy-

Mariano

greet the captain their teammate.

Great Jeter commercial with the legend Sinatra singing my way, on Derek's last special day. Fans would consider it a sin, if the yankees don't win.

Bottom of the 9th game is tied, Da Bronx crowd is in for one hell of a ride. They start to pretend, #2 will come through at the very end.

All are standing too nervous to sit, oh my lord Jeter wins the game with a clutch hit.

Fans and teams are delirious going wild while Derek and them cry tears of joy, dreams are real from a little boy.

Trayvon Goes Out For A Walk

Neighborhood watcher is on the prowl lets see who do I stop, the problem is you're not a trained cop.

You get on your phone, real cops tell you leave him alone.

You feel your bold, don't obey orders and stalk a seventeen-year-old. You got the gun, just like a bully looking for fun.

We find out teenagers name is Trayvon whose walking to the store, your names Zimmerman he's up to something you feel sure.

Trayvon turns around what does he see, some clowns following me.

They get into a fight Trayvon seems to be the winner, Zimmerman's lawyer makes the teenager out to look sinister.

Trayvon has no gun or knife, gets shot why God and loses his life.

I ask on this tragic shameful night what was Zimmerman's plan, turns out the stalker couldn't. fight and wasn't much of a man.

12 Jurors showed they are brain dead, when the verdict is read. Shameful disgrace Zimmerman as won, the persecutor with a gun.

Oh lord comfort Trayvon's parents of this wicked crime, they lost their innocent son a second time.

Acrostic Poetry

Dance smooth elegant steps and a dreamer just like me.

Always in my heart my soul sings when i see my beauty.

Unequivocal your participation fighting against cancer.

God bless you for the wonderful mother you became.

Helping special children makes you so very special at your job.

Teaching you and Peter how to dance and sing magical moments.

Everlasting love I have for you and my brilliant and beautiful grandchildren.

Remember if you need me for whatever reason I'm always here.

Marvelous mother and grandma very strict also very loving.

My Lady Mary

MARVELOUS MOM AND GRANDMA

Astonishing smile also outside beauty your warm heart even more beautiful.

Reliable always there when it counts most and giving great advice.

Yearning desire to be close to my lady, my lover, my best friend.

Alone And Out Of Sight

So much on my mind, taking a long walk don't know what I'll find.

Do that often these days late at night, deep thinker trying to make things right. Feeling so all alone, hardly ever talk to anyone on the phone.

Hear steps behind me don't seem to care, that's how I feel in this awful nightmare. Family bad news most of the time, don't enjoy writing a sad rhyme.

Getting darker streetlights so dim, questioning my choices was their too much sin. Back in the day I had it made, all those great times shame memory starting to fade.

Reminiscing seeing much family and friends every day my life has changed its gone astray. So damn lonesome hurts down deep, it's the reason I can't sleep.

Singing a Sinatra torch song, while I'm strolling along, what the hell did I do that was so wrong.

Always been an Italian romantic guy, now alone asking myself why.

I adore my loved ones so damn much, sadly to some that's not enough, oh Lord my heart is broken, this emptiness I feel my soul has spoken.

I walk this cold bitter night, so all alone and out of sight.

FROM HER EYES TO MINE

As I sit in heaven my love and watch you every day, I try to let you know with signs I never went away.

I hear you when you complain and watch you as you sleep, I always put my arms around you as you weep.

Sometimes in life your dearest friends and family will let you down, I'll put a smile back on that frown.

I see you waste the days away knowing I won't be there at our happy home, so I will make it better so you don't feel so alone.

Don't feel guilty that you have life that was denied me, heaven is truly beautiful just you wait and see.

So live your life laugh more enjoy yourself be free, then I know each and every day you'll be thinking not only of me.

As you get older, I will always be the angel on your shoulder.

Oh my Peter, my son and your son don't want to see you sad and weary, sincerely your loving Mary.

HONOR OUR MEMORIAL DAY

I dedicate this poem to my brother Louis Velotti and dear friend Mike who both fought in Korea and all who served our Country.

Today America honors all who served, which they truly deserved.

For those who went beyond the call of duty to save a fallen brother, never to come home to his grieving dad and mother.

Your vivacity for courage will shine a light, ever so very bright.

For those ingrates who show disloyalty to our flag and Country they have no clue, those rights freedom of speech and protest are because of Veterans like you.

No Vets should be homeless this should not be, you were also the guardian of our protection for all the world to see.

When you return home what a beautiful touching sight, when loved ones run your way holding you so tight.

Not so long ago vets returning home from Vietnam communist brain washed students and supporters spit in their face, imagine how they felt what a terrible disgrace.

Today thank God most of our vets are treated with respect and grace.

Many will visit cemetery's and leave our flag by someone's grave, for the honored Vets who fought so very brave.

Please Lord watch over our warriors in harm's way, while we honor our Memorial Day.

I FEEL YOUR LOVE WHEREVER I GO

I love you dad and want you to know, I feel your love wherever I go. Whenever I have problems you're there to assist, the way you have helped me would make quite a list.

Your wisdom and knowledge have shown me the way, and I'm thankful for you as I live day by day I don't tell you enough how important you are, in my universe you're a bright shining star.

All my love forever and ever your memo.

Michele Velotti

SITTING IN A LONELY ROOM

Patient sitting in a lonely room, feeling so very gloom.

Gets a call from a stranger, read about your awful accident hope your out of danger. My job in life is to make people feel better, rather a phone call than a letter.

Patients says very nice of you, I've been in this hospital room without a view. Six months since I've been outside, never no visitors at my bedside.

I love nature and long walks new friend I'll call you every other day to talk. He tells him how lovely spring looks, the sky trees mountains and brooks.

He mentions all the gorgeous colors of leaves and flowers green yellow and red, while the patient has tears of joy laying in his bed.

His friend says I pray for you every day, in my heart I know you will be ok.

He finds out he's going home, he gets another call on the phone he tells his friend thanks for Making me fight, in this dark room you brought light.

The way you see, and explain nature to me.

You made me feel I was outside every day, I can't thank you enough I truly don't know what to say.

Amazingly he finds out his friend was always blind, so many thoughts run through his minds. Overwhelmed he tells his friends wife, your husband is special and so very nice.

He explains nature so vivid it blows my mind, how was this possible if he was always blind. His wife smiles and says how very true, but the Lord allowed him to imagine better than I or you.

Its Time To Say Goodbye

Why can't we speak of someone we love and miss, you always remember the twinkle in the eyes or a simple kiss.

Feelings don't change, they are untouched they have so much range.

Is it wrong for me to say I love and miss you, oh God you know how much I do. That pain you feel in your heart will never leave, seems like forever I will grieve.

Yes there were tears of sorrow but also of tremendous joy, could be your wife mom dad in my case my wonderful boy.

No one has the right to tell me what to feel or what to say, you don't walk in my shoes every day.

Oh my son the pain is so terribly strong, I ask Lord did I do something so very wrong, many good times you your sister and I when singing a song.

Your moms love was true, her lovely face would light up looking at you two.

You were so caring and very smart, Peter your friends never forgot, you will forever remain in their heart.

Oh my beautiful son you were only fifteen, so sad never again to be seen.

I wonder are you watching over your sister friends and me, we had so much fun playing sports or reminiscing under a shady tree.

Oh sweet Lord I keep asking why why why let me dry my tears it's time to say goodbye.

To Distinguish
The Four Seasons

New York City has always been my home one of the main reasons, is has four seasons.

In the winter Manhattan lights aluminate so pretty, you can also see the Christmas show at Radio City.

Walking feeling the crunch of the snow before dark, in beautiful Central Park. Also going for a jog at a slow pace, while snowflakes caress your face.

After a cold winter the glorification of spring, just listening to the birds sing. Being on a lake to row, or a stroll in the garden to see flowers grow.

My best season is summer its my seashore time, Mary my lady the hand she holds is mine. Great feeling coaching my son after a win or watching my lovely daughter swim.

Going on a cruise laying by the pool in the sun, having so much fun. To embrace the fruition of it all, is how I feel about fall.

The Kaleidoscope and endless variety of colorful leaves, while they gently flutter from the trees.

Some say fall is more comforting that's why they like it best, just lay back close your eyes to rest.

Oh Lord I enjoy the four seasons all of the time, I have my poetry choosing prose or rhyme.

Why Is Everybody Always Picking On Me

Have you ever seen any ball player better than me or as strong, we all know I did no wrong. I am Alex Rodriguez the king, oh my what the hell happened to my swing.

I own a mansion and a $270 million dollar contract, all the women know I am more handsome and sweeter than the captain Derek Jeter.

Madonna whispered in my ear I'm the best she ever had, last night she slept with me seven brothers and their dad, I was a God always called A-rod.

I am too wonderful to have used a steroid, oh no now they call me A-roid.

I cost the Yankees many millions some fans asked why, oh no I was caught in another lie. How dare Girardi put me on the bench where's his wit, I'll show them all I'll just quit.

Please Yankee fans hear my plea, why is everybody always picking on me.

Old Photos And Other Things

There are items and mementos to which we cling, to some it doesn't mean a thing. Came across an old note, my dad reminding me to vote.

Looking at trophies covered in dust, some are even starting to rust. Old records of my older brother, what a voice he had so did my mother.

One of my five sisters kept and old love letter, I asked why always made her feel better. Looking over photo albums haven't seen for a while, such a nice feeling always makes me smile.

Many pictures of my daughter and son, thank you Lord we had so much fun.

Old birthday cards from my lady Mary they always touched my heart, so glad in my mind we are together and not apart.

For me its not strange to which we cling, looking at these lovely mementos how my heart sings for faded photos and other things.

Still Looking Gorgeous To Me

When I first laid my eyes on you I said this lady possesses so much beauty, a so-called friend said watch out she's also snooty.

She stood up straight, her walk had that perfect gate we didn't get along at first, but I wanted her I had this hunger and thirst.

She likes to play her game, no doubt she felt the same.

When I first held her close I heard a melancholy sound of soft sighs, as we gazed into each others eyes.

As our lips touched ever so softly our first kiss, was perfected bliss.

Our first-time making love was very nice, but in my heart I knew there wasn't enough spice. The second time was sizzling hot romance, we both admit we were in a magical trance.

I have always been a romantic, our jealousy at times became frantic.

Much time has passed I still love holding hands as we walk in the park, and romanticizing in sunlight or after dark.

We always loved dancing fast or slow, Lord knows I love you so. Our love was destiny, even older your still looking gorgeous to me.

Stand Up To What's Right

Two policemen murdered will Reverend Sharpton show respect, when It comes to this classless fool what did you expect.

He and professional agitators show no feelings, unlike Reverend King and Mandella he's not about healing.

When it comes to bad cops marchers had the right to shout, and demand we want them out. The putrid anti-cop Mantras we heard what you said, you chanted we want these pigs dead. Mayor DeBlasio and Sharpton should have demanded this vile speech stops, no one has the right to kill innocent cops.

Both of you are too uncaring to react, how can you blame cops for turning their back.

Even when cops are proven right this Reverend plays the race card, you suppose to be a man of God,

Mayor softy how do you make him your right hand man, its all about him that's his only plan. He owes $4 million in taxes how could this be, that's a jail sentence and fine for you and me. Lies about Tawana accused innocent man of rape, again no jail time slick Rev manages to escape.

Court and drug scandal by the FBI saying how do I let this go away, public see this on tape Rev becomes a rat this so called man of faith.

You rant and rave while two good cops go to their grave. You're not a peace maker, you're a race baiter.

When your proven wrong you have no shame, it's always the cops that you blame. People of all colors lets unite, stand up to what's right.

Close Friends Are Family To Me

Back in the day growing up Italian family dinner, always made me feel like such a winner. Magnificent Italian food and wine, loving family together all of the time.

Mom cooking five sisters sitting up my brother and I start to sing, dad at the head of the table feeling like a king.

My brother Louie always telling a joke, after dinner tv time no one spoke.

Later I got married to my lovely Janette later having two wonderful children Peter and Michelle, oh God everything went so well.

Move to Country Club new home, filled with family and friends never felt alone, sports with my son I was in a magical trance, constant music with my daughter Michelle we all loved to sing and dance.

My marriage failed my dream became a lie, most of my entire family and my only son I've watched them die.

My loving daughter Michelle and grandchildren I adore, wish I saw them more.

Only relative I talk to Anna often love her only liga left from 7 siblings how sad, this makes me so damn mad.

Closet friends now are so very few, Bobby Lucille Mike Dennis Maryann and her husband Frankie Pru.

You see, close friends are family to me.

The Loudest Noise Is Silence

I want to say, on this old winter day. Its not hard to say I'm sorry realizing both of us are not strong, to this Chicago hit song.

You don't want to hear my plea, while the rapture of sadness surrounds me. The emptiness of being alone, hoping to hear your voice on the phone.

We hurt each other with angry words and you walked away, as I listen to this love song on Valentines

Day this was always our special time, now by myself I write words that rhyme. Oh my lady I close my eyes, trying to answer all the why's.

The music sways me into a trance I pretend while I hold you very close to dance. The cold ones say a man should never cry, while my tears fall unashamed to deny. My awful words broke your heart, I the romantic not very smart.

You've taken me for granted is so unkind, I can't get it out of my mind. Changing the song to Billy Joel, your name is written on my soul.

Holding hands walking in the park I felt blessed, now all I feel is loneliness.

God knows I'd never raise my hand to you I don't phantom that type of violence, strange the loudest noise is silence.

Oh Lord Can't I Ever Go Home

Dedicated to my nephew Louis Liga

I went to visit my nephew Louie in what is called an old age home, looking at him and others that looked so very alone.

So this is what we do to our love ones, please hear me daughters and sons. It's visiting hours I'm the only one here, this isn't right it's so damn unfair.

Same old lines what's up my man how you doing, Yankees game on their losing.

My nephew looks up hi Uncle Peter with his sad eyes, strange all the forgotten have that same look when visitors say their goodbye.

The usual conversation how the food today, sadly he never has much to say. Where's your roommate he got lucky and died from this prison gate.

I know this sounds mean, for every individual this is no fucked up dream.

We talked of our once large family always together, ones that are left don't visit bad or good weather.

This is considered a good home, hardly ever get a call on their damn phone.

Nurses give them good care and bring some joy, some show appreciation others feel it's only a ploy.

Family drop off new roommate he looks so gloom, he sobs I gave you a home all I get is a little room.

They leave shakes his hand not even a hug, he tells them I feel like a used rug.

No compassion they reply dad we will call you on the phone, head down he cries oh Lord can't I ever go home.

Oh Lord Can't I Ever Go Home (Continued)

My nephew asked why no girl ever loved him, he said that she didn't have to be beautiful just feminine.

I know I'm autistic not too smart, but uncle I have a good sensitive heart.

With Tears in my eyes I kissed his cheek unable to speak I left that room, of so much gloom.

Dedicated to my niece Anna Liga

Always has my back. Love her dearly.

Nice respectable and loving. Especially her children and grandchildren.

Nervy as little as she is and awful Italian temper. A fighter.

Affectionate warm regards to elderly and close friends. So proud of her in the way she fought her demons.

No one showed more respect and love toward my lady. Always refer to her as my Aunt Mary. These two are what family is all about.

Dedicated to my second wife Sonia Alva Velotti

S-panish passionate lover. Adorable expressive eyes that talk.

O-utstanding loving family that I respect and adore.

N-ever raise my hand to you, but I hurt you deeply. SHAME ON ME!

I-ntelligent. Fights for what she believes in.

A-ppreciation of things that matter. Sensitive awareness.

Always there when needed especially for her daughter Michelle and my son Peter.

That magical moment that made your lovely face and heart burst with pure ever lasting joy with special

words from my son's huge heart.

Sonia You Don't Have A Son I'll Be The Son You Never Had!

You were motionless with falling tears from your expressive eyes. The pride I felt had no words in the dictionary.

Is It Really Over?

Could not wait for this playoff to begin, the way my yankees are playing I consider this a sin. Every fans face has a frown when Derek Jeter went down.

Oh no, no, lost again two games to go.

Just lost another how could this be, oh Lord that makes three.

Come on Yankee fans lets stand and shout, we know what winning is all about. Watching this must game all alone, so called fans on their cell phone.

Those aren't the true fans I knew, these clowns don't have a clue.

Alex Rodriguez taken out played lousy should be called A-roid, he ain't much without steroids. Getting into the fourth game Detroit can't bring out the broom, oh God that's too much gloom.

No way I have faith, CC will throw strikes over the plate.

I'm from East Harlem moved to the Bronx my street and company name is Glover, fight hard This fourth game will never be over.

What just took place? I am stunned we have been swept, true yankee fans would have wept. Thinking back to East Harlem my buddies Petey Fat - Dennis The Head – Champ -Philly Chich -

Petey – Duke and Sonny, this game wasn't all about the money.

I should have watched an old movie with Rod Steiger, we just got bit by a tiger.

Can't imagine Micky – Roger – Yogi – Whitey and Elston fans reigning down with booze, my guys Hated to lose.

I have to face it its not the same, Yankee pride they would have felt the shame. Oh those memories all the joy, when I Frank Prudenti was the yankee bat boy.

Is It Just Coincidental?

Non believers feel there are no such things as spirits or angels how do you explain these incidents.

Around five months after my Petey's passing, I was driving alone late at night. All of a sudden his passing truly hit me.

Before this moment I was a zombie, never truly accepting my only son was dead. I started sobbing like never before, screamed out his name.

Put my foot down on the petal not knowing what the hell I was doing my car was up to 120.

Thank God very few cars on the highway so late at night. Innocent people would have been killed and myself.

All of a sudden I felt a soothing hand on mine, and then a soft voice near my ear Saying "Dad What Are you Doing Please Pull Over" of course I listened.

I ask is it just coincidental? Was it my sons spirit or angel? My Peter had four close friends who he considered brothers; Rubin Casado, George Czerniewski, lieutenant Colonel Cuva and Former Police officer Jason Medina.

Rubin crying, said that he was in his darkest moments doing things that he knew his best friend would

be ashamed of, when he felt Peters presence that changed his life around. Is it just coincidental?

George and I, at my sons grave, I mention often when I'm here alone, I look up in the sky, and birds fly directly over me.

Well out of no where, seconds after that remark directly over our heads birds appear George looks at me and said that's our Peter's spirit.Is it just coincidental?

John Cuva said often when he and his men were attacked and things look very dim he would pray to the Lord and he also prayed to his best friend Peter and he would feel

Is It Just Coincidental? (Continued)

His presence.

The firing would stop. Is it just coincidence?

Former police officer Jason said often when fired upon in the south Bronx things would get so very

dangerous often I felt Peter over my shoulder and it made me feel safe. Is it just coincidental? My wife Sonia and I were going on my favorite ride at Disney World a year after my son past. As we approach out of nowhere a beautiful rainbow over this particular ride.

How strange for more than an hour before it never rained. We looked at each other with Happy tears in our eye we knew Peter was with us to go on his and our favorite ride.

Is that just coincidental?

On my sons birthday I just left the cemetery to visit my nephew Many Liga in the hospital. His daughters were in the room.

My nephew was in a coma for over a week with no hope we were talking stories of how their dad always made my son and my lady Mary laugh those three loved each other dearly.

All of a sudden, Many raised his arm and opened his hand.

His eyes never opened I put my hand in his he took four deep breaths and passed. We started hugging and crying.

His wife Rua-rey entered the room screaming oh no Many why couldn't you wait for me? When her children Michelle and Denise explained what she missed, she came up to me and grabbed my face putting it so close to hers and said "Oh My God Your Angel Peter On His birthday came for my husband to take him to heaven".

The Doctors I spoke to had no explanation how someone in a coma had that reaction to lift his arm and open his hand.

Is it just coincidental? Soar Soar my angels. Open your wings and soar.

Now Stop The Madness

Answers now no more pretense, we all demand percep1on and common sense. I believe in the second amendment, only to a certain extent.

To expend in a particular direction becomes trend, if proven to be ques1onable debate them, family or friend.

The NRA has done just that by allowing rapid fire weapons to be sold its not reasonable, not to the children would be inexcusable.

We all must hear what they are saying they the victimized, have truly been traumatized.

Law enforcement and NRA are correct gun free zones are insecure and total insanity, statistics prove its so much easier for evil to strike each vicinity.

Forget politics left or right, we must join together to do what's right.

Our great minds who wrote the second amendment of diligent instructions, never dreamed of weapons of mass destruction.

Does any serious-minded person feel they would want disturbed vicious people carrying such arsenal, that would be insensible.

Where is the vision, so much violence in Hollywood movies music video games and television.

Foolish excuses religious fana1cs use explosives and trucks not always guns, tell that to our murdered daughters and sons.

All schools must have metal detectors and trained guards to be safe, if not evil will come to each and every place.

Unlike our many heroic cops and firefighters four deputy sheriffs hid instead of going in, such gutless interaction.

Vicious intruders are armed that's their security.

Our students and teachers need us to stand tall, God bless them all. No more excuses enough of too much sadness, now stop the madness.

✳ No Need To Lock The Door Anymore ✳

Punishment started at age six her stepdad took away her favorite toy, shouting "be like your brother he's a good boy."

As she got older her life became much worse, "she was told you are a curse." When she reached eight, in her older brothers eyes she saw such hate.

When her mom and brother spoke up for her they would be abused, now she was so Afraid and confused.

Now eleven, her mom dies brother tells her "she's free and in heaven."

Brother stands up for his sister every day, stepdad sends him to live with relatives far away. Now alone the low life pig whispers in her ear, "your quite sexy my dear."

I know bitch you liked what I said, as he lifted her on the bed. He did sexual acts often in that room, of so much gloom.

Always too frightened to move and in so much pain, she felt she was going insane. He told her she's a bad girl and don't tell if so you go to hell.

She called her brother crying and shaking telling she locks her door every day, praying her stepdad will go away. She yells I'm so ashamed, am I the one to blame.

He promised her the evil will stop soon, I will be there tomorrow afternoon. That night her putrid stepdad was found dead, wrist cut in his blood soaked bED.

continued

Cops protecting the brother claimed suicide note which read "No need to lock the door, anymore."

I Love You Dad

I love you dad and want you to know, I feel your love wherever I go.

Whenever I have problems you're there to assist, the ways you have helped me would make quite a list.

Your wisdom and knowledge have shown me the way, and I'm thankful for you as I live day by day.

I don't tell you enough how important you are, in my universe you're a bright shining star. All my love forever and ever your memo

Written by Michele Velotti

Respected And Appreciated

You my Peter V opened my soul to kindness and love I never knew

Your sisters and brother opened their arms and heart that brought such happy tears. I foolishly got married way too young.

My children Daphne, Jr and Jermaine were a blessing. My love for them has no words.

Their wonderful children made this grandma young again. Watching them grow, as you say made my heart sing.

If it weren't for my children, I would have taken my life from all the beatings and verbal abuse in a marriage of hell.

As you were told by coworkers many times I wore sunglasses on the job to hide my bruises. What that monster did gave me the power to leave him.

You my love brought me out of the darkness and despair. You are such an important part of me.

It's difficult to express the changes you brought to my mind and heart.

Words do not do justice to my emotions when I want you, need you, and most of all love you with every breath of my being.

When I look at you, I see a man who knows the difference between actions and words.

I see a man whose brave enough to meet challenges and humble enough to admit mistakes. In the beginning making love to you was so very passionate and breathtaking.

Now the romance still feels special just holding hands, kissed tenderly, or wrap ourselves into each others arms.

No doubt we argued with that Italian temper of yours and me being an angry black woman who takes no bs.

Oh my passionate lover it's been a wonderful emotional joy ride. All the traveling, concerts, and dances.

Can't imagine having shared with anyone else but you my love. You gave me such splendor to feel appreciated my love.

Respected And Appreciated (Continued)

✱ Goodbye is not forever ✱

My lady your first birthday in heaven twenty-nine years we would celebrate your special day, how do I do that now that you are away.

You always knew, how very much I loved you.

My daughter Michele said you were the strongest lady she ever knew, how right she was I am lost without you.

You were my diamond in the rough, so strong so tuff.

Five months seems like such a long while, oh my lady how I miss your beautiful smile. Tears I keep wiping away, such a sad way to celebrate your birthday.

We had glorious plans to party with friends and family on this 5th day of September, that's what I'll always have to remember.

Now I will just pretend we are holding each other close on the dance floor, oh why Lord never to be no more.

Can't fathom the thought I will spend your birthday alone, your last words "be strong my love on the phone."

You my gorgeous lady Mary Alice Miller look so forward to today, so sad you were taken away. Over 150 celebrating for you would have been so swell, at the beautiful Surf Club in New Rochelle.

Goodbye is not forever goodbye is not the end, it simply means we will miss each other terribly until we meet again.

Mysterious

What's on your mind, I seem to be thinking that all the time.

When it comes to you I boast, because you come through for me the most. It was different before, I know in my heart I love you more.

Too often we argue over nothing, you obviously feel it's something.

You continue to have an attitude, when I answer back you claim I'm rude.

This leads to both of us getting very mad, then we mope around feeling quite sad.

I call you and ask would love to see you more, your ridiculous uncaring reply what for.

My lady we have done so much together, when we talk of the past times were so much better. I love you I know I always will, wondering do you feel the same still.

Of course at times I know I'm wrong, I know in my heart my love for you is strong. At times I get delirious, asking myself why is she so damn mysterious.

Where Are The So Called Fathers

Headlines Child or innocent teenager killed by mistake wrong place wrong time, lawyer tells us we should feel sorry for this slim.

He grew up in a rough place, not a trace of remorse on his face.

Where is the human spirit the perception of feeling, while the victims mother screams "oh God no" in the gutter kneeling.

Too many kids look up to gang leaders and especially drug dealer they think they're cool, if you feel for this scum you are a fool.

Drug pushers feel they deserve respect, he is nothing but a crawling insect.

Where are these so-called dads who leave home, no support for mom and kids who feel so all alone.

Main reason why kids join gangs they want to feel they belong, so called dad you are so so very wrong.

When are more people going to stand up, take notice how many politicians are corrupt.

Too many religious leaders craving to be on TV protest and holler, shame is these phonies are about the old mighty dollar.

Get involved see what's happening behind closed doors, some of these children are yours. These low life bastards that run the streets, how often they make good people weep.

Too many good families pleading for the Lord to hear their prayers they don't ask why or when, these poor trapped souls know it's going to happen again.

We see so many innocent wonderful children bleeding on the street while he or she dies, people let the streets have eyes.

Why are good people forced to live in fear, show our children protection and that we truly care.

People stand up and show these punks what we are all about, heroin and crack dealers get the hell out!

Over 90% of men in jail main reason never knew their dad uncaring even to bother, I ask again were are you so called father.

My Grandchildren

I cherish the moments when you were young, Chris and Nick we had so much fun.

My lady Mary asked don't these two ever take a nap, while you guys laid farts on her lap. Chris I taught how to play baseball you became a great hitter, didn't love the game but you weren't a quitter.

Girls loved you in your uniform said you looked adorable and he loved every second of it, Nicky you said no way baseball is boring and deplorable.

Nick driving you to high school was also a lot of fun, playing pool against you two damn you Guys were good but hardly ever won.

Chris seeing you on the stage playing drums was such a blast damn time goes by so fast. Nick while other kids would party your loving mom and I took you to karate.

Chris as a little boy you would call me to tell you a story every day, you'd rather do that than play.

When Samantha was born, in mom and Franks eyes she could do no wrong. I loved how she would boast, which brother she loved the most.

Samantha now 15 would ask how old do I have to be to go on my first date, her dad and I would say age 28

Now I watched your daughter Taylor run she is so quick, she runs faster than you or Nick. As a 5-year-old she is so very smart enthusiastic and keen, sounds more like a child of 13.

Watching you and her mom Kait play with her handsome brother Lucas is such fun, while they laugh and run.

I look at my daughter no mom or I ever loved her children and grandchildren more, that's for damn sure.

My daughters mom Jeanette and Kait and wonderful parents Judy and Dave Graney and daughter

Karriann feels the same way, as we all watch Taylor and Lucas play.

You my grandchildren even a simple thing like pushing you on a swing, would make my heart sing.

We All Must Unite

Today we see too much strife, in our way of life.

Headline cop shoots unarmed black man, if the cop is guilty all good people should take a stand.

Most cops do a great job, but some are bad and fail, they must go to jail.

Innocent good cops are being murdered at an alarming rate, fair minds have to come together in good faith.

Too many marches not the ones marching in peace are shouting kill the pigs in a blanket now That is justice, please tell me how.

Ignorant haters of both races want race riots and killing of more police, not understanding and peace.

These pathetic race baters only see chaos and hate, they will never preach of love and faith. Let's not make the separatist win, that would be a terrible sin.

Division is their goal, the devil is in their soul.

Great men Abe Lincoln and Rev. Dr. Martin Luther King spoke of equality character love right And wrong, which makes our nation strong.

Let us embrace the glorious words of these two men of grace and class, lets come together don't let their dreams just pass.

We must stop the stupidity of looking at the color of ones face, let's all be a credit to the human race.

America and the entire world do what's right, God help us we all must unite.

Found Together

I walk late at night so the darkness will hide me, tears streaming down my face for no one to see.

Our music can't play, oh Lord don't take her away. If you're out of sight, there's nothing left to write.

I can't hide my deep feeling for my lady our life should have ended like the movie "The Notebook"

Found together lying side by side until our last breath I would have held my Queen close and gently

caress her neck keep whispering in her ear of the deep love in my soul I felt for my glorious Mary.

I would be wiping away your tears as you grieved for your splendid son Jermaine. Holding you extra close kissing your luscious soft lips until the very end.

Looking deep into each other's passionate eyes still so very in love.

One last glorious moment to see your beautiful smile as we fade away into the night my lady together forever.

I Pretend You're Still Here

The glorious day you were born, my life took a new form. When I was told it's a boy, my heart burst into utopian joy. Mom and I took you home, we called everyone on the phone.

First time I held you in my arms could life get better than this, oh Lord I was in heavenly bliss.

Oh thank you God for my beautiful healthy boy, I was like a child playing with his first toy. Seeing you near your sister Michele who was 5, I felt so blessed to be alive.

Years later in the park and pushing my children on the swing, splendor I felt my heart sing. Watching you two grow what a glorious time, everything seemed to rhyme.

Us three would always sing and dance, I was in a happy trance.

O.L.A was your school, you studied hard never played the fool. Honor student was your game, so proud you had my name.

Became your manager in baseball, watching you I felt ten feet tall. Told you were too small to go far, you became a seven-time all-star.

More important you cared for kids who did not have a friend, bullies called them nerds you Would not bend.

My son gave them a head start till this day they hold you dear in their heart. Jason and you made a rap CD such cool rhymes, about those 80's times.

Amazingly you two took a spiritual name the resurrection, got the lyrics down to perfection. Now fourteen and strong, you start feeling sick somethings terribly wrong.

Doctor tells us my precious son is very ill, no no this can't be God's will.

Four months Rubin and George his two closet friends attend the hospital every day, they Comfort their buddy in such a special way.

These three are truly brothers, they tell me in tears if I lose my son I add to others. Nurses cherish my boy they say he's always trying to help, younger cancer victims looking after their health.

My Peter's handsome face and body is now so very thin, oh my Lord he's so very good why him?

I Still Pretend You're Here (Continued)

Please God hear my plea, don't take my only boy, take me.

We are told Peter's chances are very slim, while the Bronx girls and Boys pray for him. The pain becomes unbearable how could this be so.

He fought so hard his mom cries no more my son let go.

I and my wife Sonia keep caressing my beautiful boy in his hour of death, while the tears flow as my son takes his last breath.

I'm overwhelmed with sadness and hate this horrific moment unlike my son I lose my faith. All of a sudden amazingly a peaceful look on my Peter's face, this must be the good Lords grace.

My adorable precious son I swear, time passes I'll always pretend you're still here.

Us Three Were Pure Gold

Dedicated to Jennifer Velotti and Jeanette Costello Distefano

Two people who I literally worshipped as a teenager where my older brother Louie and Johnny D Distefano.

They were best friends.

My brothers girlfriends was John's sister Rosalea.

Our greatest passions were singing, listening to music constantly and East Harlem street sports.

Baseball and going to concerts seeing the greatest talent ever. The marvelous thing we did most was laugh.

Amazingly we never had an argument debate yes one other thing was practical jokes with my nephew Bobby Liga.

Oh Lord our fun together was pure gold.

My first girlfriend was Jeanette Distefano, John's sister.

Louie John and I teamed up with other singers, and African American named Slick Wallace and Abe Lopez a Puerto Rican.

People who heard us thought we were so good, that we would make it big someday. That dream never happened when the music changed.

Later on my brother became my best man at my wedding and John and usher.

Louie became God father to my daughter Michele and Johnny God father to my son Peter. When I got married a second time to Sonia Alva I asked Johnny to be my best man.

His reply I'm so ashamed because I'm short on funds and I won't be able to give you an expensive gift.

My reply "Johnny you are the gift".

Oh yeah looking back us three those glorious times were pure gold.

Hey guys give my lady Mary and son Peter and my five sisters mom and dad a song just for me.

My Stepsons
By My Side

In Honor of Rubin Casado and George Czerniewski

My Peter became friends with Rubin at seven-year-old, when my son extended his hand to a nervous Rubin on his first day in class.

Rubin said at that precise moment they became best friends.

Played little league baseball, they spend many summer vacations with Rubin's loving mom Hadee.

George also played little league baseball with Peter. Me being manager of these two was pure gold.

George lost his mom at 11 years old.

At 14 I took my son and George to Disney World with my daughter Michele and second wife Sonia Alva.

We all had a blast.

Rubin and Peter spent time together with their first girlfriends at 14 years old.

Sadly at 14 my son was diagnosed with cancer these two youngsters as soon as they heard the awful news were at my boys side.

Giving him hope and praying so very hard, as well all his many Bronx friends.

In the hospital for four months these two 14 year olds visited their best friends bedside just about every day.

Peter became very thin and we were given the worst news any parent would want to hear. Your son has only a few weeks left.

No words in the dictionary could possibly explain how Peter's mom Janette and my daughter felt.

A good part of me died that very moment.

I didn't tell Rubin or George he had no hope, but these two young men knew in their hearts it looked

very grim for their best friend.

On the way out of the hospital Rubin and George with tears in their eyes told me words that caressed.

My Stepsons By My Side (Continued)

my heart and soul this many years later.

"If your Peter our brother doesn't make it you lose one son but you gain two others." Wow when my beautiful boy passed these two best friends gave the eulogy inside O.L.A Church.

George did a touching beautiful poem called "Best friends".

Rubin wrote words from his heart both eulogies had everyone listening and in tears.

My dad sitting near me was sobbing, and said these two aren't boys, they just became men. My stepsons I'm sure you realize your brother my glorious boy had a big smile on his face and was proud of his two brothers.

You two, with Sonia, were my right arm. The love I feel for you makes my heart sing.

When I close my eyes I see you John Cuva, Tommy Neglia, Anthony Luciano, Lippolis Brothers on those field of dreams with all my other wonderful players.

Rubin George my Peter will always live in our hearts.

Thank you both from the bottom of my soul for being at my side and at your brothers.

My Two Hero's

Dedicated to Natasha Agard and Jalin Cave Miller

Family and close friends are so very important, especially when they're needed in a crises. Natasha and Jalin did just that.

My lady had just lost her wonderful youngest son Jermaine, Jalin's dad, Natasha's uncle. Covid sadly took Jermaine's life.

My lady at this time had it also mildly.

Natasha showing such loving care and courage took care of her grandma at home. They loved each other dearly.

Often the phone would ring, Mary would say to me, "its my Tosh" my lady's nickname for her. They would talk for hours of her beautiful granddaughters life problems.

My lady was a great listener, as good a mom and grandma that ever walked the face of this earth.

Just ask her son Jr. who called his mom "my girl".

Jr. and I would call often to see how his mom was doing. Jr. worshiped the ground his loving mom walked on.

My lady would tell me, oh Peter my Tosh is doing everything possible to comfort me. I love her so very much I'm so afraid she might get sick also.

Nursing me day and night.

My lady's condition got worse, she was rushed to the hospital when I would call her, you could barely hear her voice.

In a gentle whisper she told me she could hardly breath and hoped I could be close to her in her hour of need.

She also mentioned how she would rather have Tosh nursing her instead of strangers adding, she missed me and her children and grandchildren so very much.

My lady's condition was not getting any better as she mentioned to me I need my daughter Daffney.

Have to talk to her and Jr. no matter how old they are there still my babies. She kept saying both their names over and over especially her loving daughter.

Then she sobbed why did the Lord take my baby Jermaine he was so so very good.

My Two Hero's (Continued)

His beautiful children need him everybody loved him. He had so much to give.

I don't know if I can go on I feel so very sad and weak.

I and her son Jr. would constantly tell her to fight please don't give up.

The last call I got from my beautiful lady she in a whisper said, "I'm ready you must be strong my love".

I pleaded "oh no my baby without you there is no me."

She said I'm so sad now I know how you feel in losing a son. Fifteen days have passed since Jermaine passing.

Natasha called me and said "Peter I love you". I screamed out loud "Mary Mary."

I knew at that second my beautiful lady was gone.

A good part of me died with her in that very deep sad awful moment.

Natasha the love and respect I feel for you in my soul will last until my last breath. God bless you.

In The funeral home Jr. Little B Bryant and I arrived way before the family.

Once our eyes saw mom and son's coffin side by side we laid our heads on them and cried uncontrollably.

Jr. pulled up a chair very close as I held him from behind. Natasha Jalin and I gave Eulogies.

Jalin's mom Erika took the podium and stated with eyes tearing how proud she was of her loving son

Jalin who stepped up like a man and took care of family business.

Jalin's father Jermaine was a remarkable caring soul a true class act. Jalin I'm proud to say takes right after him.

Both excelled at basketball, but even ore in the way they care for others especially the Queens Boys and Girls of Rochdale Village.

Jermaine Gave his time effort and money in starting basketball camps for hundreds of youngsters.

His brother in law Larry Cave and niece former basketball all star Christina Krystina Agard

My Two Hero's (Continued)

Little B were also deeply involved with coaching and so many other important other duties. Jalin played and also coached younger kids.

Maine Loved his job as Director at "Sheltering Arms" for children.

Jermaine said over 90% didn't know their dads so he dedicated his time to them so they could stay out of trouble.

The family and community bonding of Rochdale village was so very special.

Since Jermaine's passing his son Jalin is going to carry his dad's wonderful legacy. So much like his dad, this smart handsome young man has such class and admires.

When Jermaine, his mother and I would talk Maines eyes would always sparkly talking about his son Jalin and beautiful daughter Jayana, so very smart also and what a personality.

Jalin's aunt Darlene also a former basketball great adores her Jalin and Jayana her love for them is so very special.

No doubt in my mind Jalin will make his dad proud and his grandma.

I always knew in my heart you would turn out to be a wonderful young man. You make us all so very proud.

You like my son Peter and your dad put a smile on God's face, not because of your accomplishments it's that you have a huge caring heart.

You three my Lady and Natasha are pure gold. I love you.

Now my lady Mary and Jermaine soar my angels soar, spread your wings together to heaven We were all blessed to have you two beautiful souls in our lives.

PRIDE

In honor of my family

The school of life is what I learned from my dad, my mom and my older brother. My mom taught me the importance of being gentle with females feelings.

She said never to put anyone down.

Dad had four main ones he talked about often.

First, never raise your hand to a woman, fight against racism, stand up to bullies and never shame him.

My brother taught me music, baseball, sex and laughter.

The most important for me is all three practiced what they preached especially against prejudice, when I was 10 years old my mother invited coworkers to dinner.

They were a mixed group of Jewish, African American and Puerto Rican.

They all had a fun time laughing and praising my mom's Italian cooking and adored her singing.

Next day in my dads club a huge handout on 118th street with game machines and gambling in the back of the store.

One of the guys playing cards said out loud "why the hell would you and your wife invite those kinds of people in your home."

My dad was very good with his hands and had a bad Italian temper.

He told this racist prick to get up and then proceeded to kick his ever-loving ass I was so damn proud,

and so was my mom when she heard what her husband did.

My five sisters and my brother when they heard this news, they all went over to my dad and gave him a big hug and kiss.

My brother Louie while at Fort Knox Kentucky during basic training in 1951 decided to go to town.

12 New York buddies, some were black and Puerto Rican this bus was full only two were able to sit,

My brother Louie being one of them.

A black woman who happened to be pregnant got on at this time some of his fellow soldiers had seats.

Pride (Continued)

Not noticing his black buddies was sitting behind a white line.

Louie stood up and offered the lady his seat, the redneck bus driver stopped the bus and shouted "hey boy what the hell do you think you're doing"?

Louie bewildered said "what's the big deal I'm giving my seat to a lady."

Bus driver goes a few blocks stops and tells two city patrol men what just happened.

The older cop demands my brother to get off, looks him over, points to his name and ask "is that an

Italian name?" My brother proudly said "yes" with his New York accent.

The cop with his Southern drawl said "I bet you're from NY and adds 'down here dago we don't stand for shit".

My brother says "where I come from a real man with class stands up for a lady no matter what especially a pregnant one".

The racist asshole yells at Louie "if it weren't for that uniform which I respect I'd crack your open."

My brother says this Italian American and his black brother infantry soldiers are going to fight in Korea

and some of us won't be coming back.

The younger cop amazingly said "he's got a great point, it's ok get back on the bus."

His fellow soldiers applaud what he does, including some of the passengers who were white. This story was told to me from a friend of my brothers named Govan who was a soldier on that bus.

They became postal police together. Govan use to call me little fanculo.

Their friendship lasted over 40 years and Govan sometimes had Sunday dinner with my family In East Harlem and the Bronx.

Govan just so happened to be black.

Like I said Im very proud to be a part of the Velotti family.

About The Author

My name is Peter Velotti.

Born in East Harlem. Moved to da Bronx. Now reside in New Rochelle, NY. Two children, Michele and Peter, sadly at 15, he passed.

Married their loving mom Jeanette, divorced. Married Sonia Alva. Divorced also.

Dear friend today. Parents, five sisters and brother, all passed, including 5 nephews and nieces.

In 2020 I also lost my stepson to covid, Jermaine, 15 days later his mom, my lady Mary A. Miller also died. Why God?

Blessed to have 3 grandchildren; Chris, Nick and Samantha. I also have 2 great grandchildren: Taylor and Lucas.

I am a retired postal worker. Became a Poet-Actor with dear friend Charlie Giardino, also deceased.

So you can see many sad awful moments in my journey thru life, but also many glorious moments. Having them in my life was pure gold. Had two poems published in 2016 called, "Famous Poets Of

The Heartland". One of those poems about Whitney Houston called, "That Glorious Voice", which took first place.

I've had many gigs in the village, in Manhattan to da Bronx and many other States. I've been on radio often, also college and universities.

In acting, started as a teenager in a high school musical, the great "West Side Story". I played the part of a kid named Action.

In the last few years, did 2 shorts and a featured film called "The Dash". This independent film won Best Actor for writer Chris Raffaele. Actor Tim Cinnante was also great in it.

My poetry is in many varieties and styles. My stories also come from a deep place in my heart.

My other passion was singing R & B and Doo-Wop with many different groups. I managed my son in little league baseball, he was an All Star 7 straight years.

Hope you enjoy my creativity on these pages, which brought so many tears I could fill an ocean. My wish, is it brings a specific emotional response that caresses your heart, and also brings a smile that brings you back to a moment in time that was special in your life. I also write about the streets of NYC and da Bronx, racisms, injustice, separatism is another very important issue, family, close friends, laughter, music and sports surrounded my world - losing so very many of my loved one's has brought so much agony and deep pain. To get up from my knees.

"I Pretend You're Still Here"

Made in the USA
Middletown, DE
23 July 2021